# Symphony No. 5
## in C-sharp Minor

## Gustav Mahler

DOVER PUBLICATIONS, INC.
Mineola, New York

*Bibliographical Note*

This Dover edition, first published in 1998, is an unabridged republication of *Symphonie No. 5 für grosses Orchester,* originally published by C. F. Peters, Leipzig, 1904. An instrumentation list and a glossary of German terms have been added.

*International Standard Book Number: 0-486-40115-4*

Manufactured in the United States of America
Dover Publications, Inc., 31 East 2nd Street, Mineola, N.Y. 11501

CONTENTS

# Symphony No. 5
## in C-sharp Minor
(1901–1904)

*Instrumentation*     *iv*
*Glossary of German Terms*     *v*

## I

## II

## III

# INSTRUMENTATION

4 Flutes [Flöten]
*Flutes 3 & 4 double Piccolos 1 & 2* [Piccolo-Flöte]

3 Oboes [Hoboen]
*Oboe 3 doubles English Horn* [Engl. H.]

3 Clarinets in C, A, B♭ ("B") [Klarinetten, Klar.]
*Clarinet 3 doubles D Clarinet* [D-Klar.]

Bass Clarinet in A, B♭ ("B") [Basskl.]

3 Bassoons [Fagotte, Fag.]

Contrabassoon [Contraf(agott), C-Fagott]
*Doubles Bassoon 3*


6 Horns in F [Hörner]
4 Trumpets in F, B♭ [Trompeten, Tromp.]
3 Trombones [Posaune, Pos.]
Tuba [Basstuba, Tuba]


Harp [Harfe]


Timpani [Pauken]


Percussion
 Glockenspiel [Glockensp.]
 Cymbals [Becken], attached to Bass Drum
 Bass Drum [Grosse Trommel, Gr. Tr.]
 Side Drum [Kleine Trommel, Kl. Tr.]
 Triangle [Triangel]
 Slapstick [Holzklapper]
 Tamtam


Violins I, II [(Erste, Zweite)Violinen, Viol.]
Violas [Violen]
Cellos [Violoncelle, Vcelle]
Basses [Bässe]

# GLOSSARY OF GERMAN TERMS

*ab,* off

*abdämpfen,* damp

*aber,* but

*absetzen,* remove

*abwechselnd,* alternating

*abwogend,* ebbing

*acht,* eight

*Achtel,* eighth-notes

*alle,* all

*alles,* everything

*allmählich, allmählig,* gradually

*als,* as, than

*altväterisch,* old-fashioned

*am,* on the, to the

*A-moll,* A minor

*an,* to

*andere,* other

*Andern,* others

*Anfang,* beginning

*angehalten,* slow

*anhaltend,* slower

*Anmerkung,* note

*Art,* manner

*atmen,* breathe

*auch,* also

*auf,* up, in the air, on, *auf G,* on the G string, *auf und abwogend,* surging and ebbing

*aufgestellt,* located, played

*Ausdruck,* expression

*ausdrucksvoll,* expressively

*ausklingen,* die away

*ausschlagen,* beat, conduct

*äusserst,* extremely

*B,* B-flat

*bedächtig,* deliberate, slow

*bedeutend,* significantly

*befestigt,* attached

*beginnend,* beginning

*beiden,* both

*belebend,* more animated

*belebt,* animated

*beruhigend,* becoming calmer

*beschleunigend,* accelerating

*bestimmt,* marcato

*bewegt,* agitated, *bewegter,* more agitated

*bezeichnet,* indicated

*bis,* up to, *bis zum,* until the

*Bogen,* bow(s), *Bögen,* bows, *Bogenwechsel(n),* change(s) of bow

*brechen,* arpeggiate

*breit,* broadly, *breiter,* long

*Dämpfer(n),* mute(s)

*das,* the

*dasselbe,* the same

*dem,* the

*den,* the

*der,* the, of the

*des,* of the

*deutlich,* clear, distinctly

*d.h.,* that is

*die,* the

*Dirigenten,* conductor

*Doppelgr.,* double stop

*drängen,* hurrying, *drängend,* stringendo, pressing, speeding up, *drängender,* faster
*drei,* three
*dreifach,* in three
*dreinfahren,* plunging forward
*drittem, drittes,* third

*eben,* just
*eilen,* hurry
*ein(e),* a
*einem,* one, *Einem,* one player
*einhaltend,* restrained
*einmal,* once, *noch einmal,* once again
*einzelne,* individual
*Empfindung,* feeling
*energisch,* energetically
*Entfernung,* distance
*erste, ersten, erster, erstes,* first
*Es,* E-flat
*etwas,* somewhat

*Fermate,* fermata
*Ferne,* distance
*festhalten,* keep
*feurig,* fiery
*Flag.,* harmonics
*fliessend,* flowing, *fliessender,* more flowing
*flüchtig,* fleeting
*flüssiger,* more flowing
*folgt,* follows
*freihängend,* suspended
*frisch,* lively, brisk
*für,* for

*ganz,* quite
*ganze,* whole
*gänzlich,* completely
*gebrochen,* arpeggiated
*gedämpft,* muted, muffled
*gehalten(er),* slower

*gemessen(em),* measured, *gemessener,* more measured
*gemessigt,* measured
*gepeitscht,* whipped
*gerissen,* cut off
*geschlagen,* struck, played
*geschliffen,* slurred, legato
*gest., gestopft,* bouché
*gestrichen,* bowed
*gesungen,* singing
*get., geteilt,* divisi
*(mit) Gewalt,* violently
*gewöhnlich(e),* ordinario, normal
*gezogen,* bowed
*gleiche,* same, even
*grell,* strident, shrill
*Griffbr., Griffbrett,* (on the) fingerboard
*grosser,* large
*grösster,* the greatest
*gut,* well

*Halbe,* (beat) half-notes
*Hälfte,* half (of a string section)
*Händen,* hands
*Hauch,* breath
*Hauptzeitmass,* main tempo
*heftig,* vehemently
*hervortretend,* prominent
*hier,* here, *von hier an,* from here on
*hoch,* high
*(in die) Höhe,* up, in the air
*Höhepunkt,* climax
*höher,* higher
*Holzrand,* wooden edge
*Holzschl.,* wooden mallet
*Holzstäbchen,* wooden stick

*im,* in the
*immer,* always, steadily, still, *immer noch,* still, *immer Halbe ohne zu drängen,* steadily beating half-notes without hurrying

*in*, to
*innigster*, most heartfelt
*ins*, to

*keck*, brazen, impudent
*klagend*, plaintive
*klingen*, ring, *klingen lassen*, let ring
*Kondukt*, cortege
*Kraft*, strength, *kräftig*, vigorously
*kurz*, short

*lang(e)*, long
*langsam*, slow, *langsamer*, slower,
♩ *etwas langsamer wie im letzten*
*Takte* ♩, ♩ somewhat slower, like ♩ in
the preceding tempo
*lassen*, let, allow to
*leidenschaftlich*, passionately
*letzten*, preceding

*m.*, with
*Mal*, time
*markato*, marcato
*markig*, precise, marcato
*mässig*, moderato, *mässigend*,
moderating
*Mediator*, plectrum
*mehrere*, several
*mehrfach*, several
*militärischer*, military
*mit*, with
*möglich*, possible

*nach*, in the, to, *Es nach E*, retune
E-flat to E
*nachlassend*, slowing
*nächsten*, next
*nächstfolgenden*, following
*natürlich*, ordinario
*nehmen*, take, change to
*nicht*, do not, not, *nicht mehr*, no longer

*nimmt*, take, change to
*noch*, more, still, *noch stärker werden*,
becoming yet louder, *noch ein*
*wenig*, slightly more
*nur*, only

*offen*, open
*ohne*, without
*Orchester*, orchestra

*Paukenschlägel(n)*, timpani mallet(s)
*Pauker*, timpanist(s)
*Pause*, pause
*plötzlich*, suddenly
*Pulte*, desks

*rascher*, faster
*rein*, precisely
*Resonanz*, près de la table
*roh*, *roher*, rough, raw
*ruhig*, calm, *ruhiger*, calmer

*Saite*, string
*sammeln*, gather
*Satzes*, movement
*Sch.*, *Schalltr.*, *Schalltrichter*, bells (of
wind instruments)
*Schlägel*, mallets
*schlagen*, beat, conduct
*schleppen*, drag, *schleppend*, dragging,
*ohne zu schleppen*, without dragging
*Schluss*, end
*schmeichelnd*, caressingly
*schmetternd*, blaring, cuivré
*schnell*, fast, *schneller*, faster
*schon*, still
*Schritt*, pace
*schüchtern*, timidly
*schwach*, weak, *schwächer*, weaker
*Schw.*, *Schwschl.*, *Schwammschlägeln*,
sponge mallets
*schwer*, heavy

*schwungvoll*, energetic
*sechs*, six
*sich beruhigend*, becoming calmer
*sind*, are
*singend*, cantabile
*so*, as
*Sord., Sordinen*, mutes
*spielen*, play, *zu spielen*, to be played
*spring. Bogen*, sautillé
*stark*, vigorously, *stärker*, more vigorously
*Steg*, bridge
*steigern(d)*, increasing
*stets, stetig*, constantly, steadily
*stimmen*, tune
*straffer*, tauter
*streng*, strict (tempo)
*Strich*, bowstroke, *Strich für Strich*, détaché
*stürmisch*, violently

*Takt(e)*, beat, tempo, *im Takt*, in tempo
*Teil*, part
*teilen*, divide, *nicht teilen*, unisoni
*(mit) Teller(n)*, clashed
*Ton*, tone, *Töne*, tones
*Trauermarsch*, funeral march
*Triole*, triplets
*Trommel*, drum

*u.*, and
*übergehen(d)*, progressing, moving to
*übernimmt*, takes, changes to
*und*, and
*ungefähr*, approximately
*unmerklich*, (almost) imperceptibly
*unten am Griffbrett*, at the bottom of the fingerboard

*Vehemenz*, vehemence
*verändern*, changing
*verklingend*, dying away

*verlöschend*, dying away
*viel*, much
*vier*, four
*Viertel*, quarter-notes
*von*, by
*vorher*, previously
*vorhin*, previously
*Vorschläge*, grace notes
*vorwärts*, (pressing) forward

*Wärme*, warmth
*wechseln*, change
*wenig*, little, *ganz wenig belebt*, only slightly more animated
*werden*, becoming
*wie*, like, as, as though
*wieder*, again, back to
*wild*, wild
*womöglich*, where possible
*wuchtig*, heavy, powerful, *wuchtiger*, more heavily
*wütend*, furiously

*zart*, tenderly, soft
*Zeit*, time, *(sich) Zeit lassen*, allow time
*zögernd*, lingering
*zu*, at, to, too
*zum*, for the, to the
*zurückhalten*, slow down, *zurückhaltend*, ritenuto
*zurückkehren*, returning
*zuvor*, previously
*zwei*, two, *zweite*, second, *zwei oder mehrfach besetzt*, using two or more instruments

*3fach*, in three, *4fach*, in four
*1., 2.(etc.)*, 1st, 2nd (etc.)

# Symphony No. 5
## in C-sharp Minor

# Symphony No. 5

## I
### 1. Trauermarsch

★ Vorschläge so schnell als möglich.
Grace notes as fast as possible.

* Vorschläge so kurz als möglich.
  Grace notes as short as possible.

*) Becken nach militärischer Art an der grossen Trommel befestigt.
   Cymbals, in military style, attached to the bass drum.

*) Einzelne gestopfte Töne sind mit + bezeichnet.
 Individual bouché tones are marked + .

C. B. *nicht*
eine 8ᵛᵃ höher!

Basses *not* an octave higher!

Anmerkung für den Dirigenten: Der Sinn dieses *rit.* ist beide Male: ein kurzes Anhalten, um zum darauffolgenden Akkorde mit grosser Wucht aussuholen.— *Die Figur selbst* muss im schnellen Tempo ausgeführt werden.

Note for the conductor: The sense of this *rit.* is, in both cases, a short pause, in order to drive toward the following chord with great force. *The figure itself* must be played in quick tempo.

*)Anmerkung für den Dirigenten: Geigen so vehement als möglich!
  Note for the conductor: Violins as vehement as possible!

**)Diese Vorschläge sind stets glissando (mit einem Finger gleitend) auszuführen.
  These grace notes are always to be played glissando (with a sliding finger).

keine Triole!
Not a triplet!

Bedeutend langsamer *(im Tempo des ersten Satzes „Trauermarsch")*.

336 **19**

19

*) Rit.=d. h. Kraft zum nächstfolgenden Accent sammeln.
 *Rit.*: that is, gather strength for the following accent.

(folgt lange Pause.)
(a long pause follows)

# II

## 3. Scherzo

*) Vorschläge so kurz als möglich.
Grace notes as short as possible.

114

NB. Die Violinen dürfen die Holzbläser nicht decken.
NB. The violins must not cover the woodwinds.

Note for the conductor: In this motive the eighth-note must always be played somewhat fleetingly and carelessly, in whatever instrument it appears; thus approximately as follows:

*) ohne das geringste dim.   **10**
without the least diminuendo.

Auch hier das Achtel flüchtig, ungefähr:
Likewise here, the eighth-note fleeting, approx.:

*11 Anmerkung für den Dirigenten. Von hier an a tempo
Note for the conductor:   From here on, *a tempo.*

NB. Anmerkung für d. Dirig: die Holzharmonie darf vom übrigen Orchester nicht „gedeckt" werden.
NB. Note for the conductor: The woodwind section should not be "covered" by the rest of the orchestra.

29

32

# III

## 4. Adagietto

## 5. Rondo-Finale

END OF EDITION